PET GERBILS

Text and photos by JEROME WEXLER

Albert Whitman & Company, Niles, Illinois

Also by Jerome Wexler
Pet Mice

Library of Congress Cataloging-in-Publication Data
Wexler, Jerome.
Pet gerbils / written and photographed by Jerome Wexler.
p.   cm.
Summary: Text and color photographs describe how to
house, feed, and handle a pair of pet gerbils and the
families they produce.
ISBN 0-8075-6523-7 (lib. bdg.)
1. Gerbils as pets—Juvenile literature.   [1. Gerbils.]
I. Title.   89-5636
SF459.G4W48   1990   CIP
636'.93233—dc19   AC

Table of Contents

What's a gerbil?

If you're looking for a cute, friendly little pet whose cage doesn't need cleaning very often, a gerbil might be just for you.

A gerbil (pronounced *JUR buhl*) is a furry desert animal about four inches long, just a little bigger than a mouse. Amazingly, there are some ways in which gerbils and human beings are alike. Both humans and gerbils are warm-blooded, grow hair, and produce milk for their young. Because of these similarities, gerbils and humans belong to a large group of living things called *mammals*.

Of course you can also think of many ways gerbils and people are different. One important difference is teeth. Unlike the incisors, or cutting teeth, of a human being, a gerbil's incisors keep growing all its life. Some other mammals whose incisors grow continuously are mice, hamsters, squirrels, guinea pigs, rats, and gophers. These animals all belong to the order of mammals known as *rodents*.

Different kinds of gerbils are found in Asia, Africa, and eastern Europe. The gerbil that is usually sold as a pet is known as the *Mongolian gerbil* because it is from the desert area of Mongolia, which is in east-central Asia.

In the wild, Mongolian gerbils are seldom seen. They stay in their desert burrows all day, hidden from the hot sun and sand. Only in the cool of the evening do they come out to gather food.

Today you can find gerbils for sale in most pet stores. Yet they were almost unknown until rather a short time ago. In 1954, twenty-two gerbils were shipped from Japan to some United States scientists. The animals were intended to be used for research, but the scientists who worked with the gerbils soon realized that the curious, gentle little animals (gerbils almost never bite) would also make excellent pets. They took some gerbils home for their children, and eventually the gerbils became popular pets.

Before you buy a gerbil

Gerbils are easy to take care of—easier, I think, than dogs, cats, birds, or even mice. But taking care of any animal is a responsibility. A pet's health and happiness are in your hands. Before buying your gerbils, you should ask yourself if you are ready to be responsible for them—not just for a week or two but for three or four years. That's about how long gerbils normally live.

There are other important questions to consider. How will the other members of the family feel about having gerbils in the house? Where will the gerbils live? Can you keep them safe from larger pets such as cats and dogs? Will you remember to feed your gerbils and clean their cage? What will you do if your gerbils have babies?

Gerbils are social animals—they like to be around other gerbils. One gerbil by itself isn't much fun to watch, and it may not even live very long. So you really should plan on purchasing a pair of gerbils. You can buy two males or two females, or, if you want to raise a family, you can buy a male and a female.

A home for your gerbils
Like mice and rats, gerbils must chew on hard objects to keep their constantly growing teeth worn down. If you let them run free in the house, they will chew up the furniture, and they might bite through an electrical cord and electrocute themselves or start a fire. It's also not a good idea to keep them in a cage made of a material they can chew through, such as wood or plastic.

Wire or glass cages make good homes for gerbils. Wire cages are lightweight and easy to clean, but litter can easily fall through the bars and scatter on the floor. And if the bars get bent so that there are large spaces between them, the baby gerbils can fall through.

Neither the litter nor the babies can escape from a glass tank, such as a fishtank. And I think it is more enjoyable to watch your gerbils through the clear sides of a glass cage than through wire bars.

7

Most ten-gallon glass aquariums have a floor area of about two hundred square inches. This is more than enough room for a pair of gerbils or even a gerbil family of ten or twelve. A ten-gallon tank weighs about eleven pounds, so you may want some help lifting and cleaning it.

If your gerbils are going to live in a glass aquarium, you will need to put a wire-mesh cover on top. This will let in plenty of fresh air and keep the animals from escaping. It will also keep other animals and small children from getting into the tank.

You will need another place to keep your gerbils while you are cleaning their cage or to use as a hospital if a gerbil gets sick and must be isolated. As a short-term home, you can use any container that has tall, slippery sides such as a pail or even the bathtub. Or you may want to purchase a second aquarium to use as temporary quarters.

Where should you keep the cage? A bedroom or a den makes an ideal spot. Don't put the cage in direct sunlight, over a radiator, in a cold garage or basement, or anywhere it may be too hot or too cold. Don't set it on the floor where it can be knocked over or in an area that is seldom used—you might forget about your pets.

In the desert, gerbils can survive extreme temperatures by burrowing underground, but in captivity they aren't comfortable if the temperature is much below sixty-five degrees F. or much above eighty-five degrees F. And like humans, they don't care for damp or drafty areas.

A clean, comfortable cage

Bedding, also called litter, must be placed on the floor of the cage to absorb urine and any water that may spill. Pet stores have a large variety of bedding, including wood chips, wood shavings, and dried, crushed corncobs. You can also make your own bedding using dried grass clippings or shredded paper. Be sure that the grass is free of pesticides and that the paper is free of any printing (some inks still contain lead, which is toxic). The bedding my gerbils seemed to like best was the wood shavings. They enjoyed chewing the shavings until they were almost as fine as sawdust.

How often do you need to clean the cage? If you have two gerbils in a ten-gallon aquarium, you will probably only need to clean it every two weeks. To be sure, just stick your nose into the cage. If it smells, you might want to clean ahead of schedule.

Put the gerbils in a safe place, then dump out the old bedding. Wash the aquarium thoroughly with a low-sudsing soap or detergent (liquid laundry detergent does a good job) and water, and rinse it well. This is also a good time to wash the waterer or any other equipment the gerbils have been using. Be sure everything is dry, then put in new bedding and return your gerbils to their home.

The waterer

Gerbils are desert animals with very efficient kidneys. They excrete only a drop or two of urine each day, and their droppings, or feces, are small, dry pellets. In the desert they obtain all the water they need from their food. They don't drink much water in captivity, but they learn to like it, and it should be supplied at all times.

If a dish of water is placed in the cage, it will either quickly fill with litter so the water has to be replaced or spill so you have to put down new bedding. The best way of supplying gerbils with water is to use a gravity-feed waterer. Several types can be found in pet stores. I recommend the type that has a tube fitted with a small ball at the drinking end. When a gerbil wants a drink, it pushes the ball up with its tongue or teeth, and a small droplet of water comes out. The waterer hangs from the top of the cage, and it should be adjusted so that the gerbils can easily reach the drinking tip.

Because gerbils drink so little, a filled waterer can last as long as two months. But you should give your pets fresh water at least every week, and wash the waterer every two weeks, when you clean the cage. Use a bottle brush and hot water and soap. Rinse it well.

What do gerbils eat?

In the wild, gerbils eat almost anything they can find—seeds, leaves, grasses, fruits, and even an insect if they can catch one. You should try to feed your pet gerbils a similar diet.

Many pet stores sell seed mixes made for mice, gerbils, and hamsters. If you can't find such a mix, you can purchase a combination made for canaries or wild birds. With any seed mix, it's best to remove most of the sunflower seeds, which are rich in oil and high in calories. Gerbils love sunflower seeds, but too many will make them fat. Save a few and use them as rewards when you train your animals.

Some animal feed companies grind seeds and other nutritious ingredients, add vitamins and minerals, and compress the mixture into hard pellets. The pellets come in all shapes and sizes— for small animals like gerbils and mice and for larger animals like dogs. You can buy pellets in pet stores.

A diet of pellets is likely to be well balanced, and because the pellets are very hard and require a lot of chewing, they help keep gerbils' teeth in shape. But not all gerbils like pellets—many prefer plain seed. A supply of both always should be kept in the cage.

In addition to seeds or pellets, you should feed your gerbils something from the plant world every day—a small piece of lettuce, kale, spinach, broccoli, celery, carrot, potato, apple, pear, etc. After ten minutes you should remove all uneaten plant food from the cage. Any left may spoil and make your gerbils sick.

If you wish, you can also feed your gerbils an insect two or three times a month. I recommend only one kind of insect—live crickets purchased at a pet store. These crickets are raised to be fed to insect-eating animals. They are free of all chemicals and pesticides which might harm your pet. So, please, don't feed your gerbils flies, caterpillars, or earthworms—only crickets from a pet store.

I always keep a piece of dog biscuit in the cage. Dog biscuits are high in protein, and like the pellets, they help wear down gerbils' ever-growing teeth.

Although you may be tempted occasionally to give your gerbils a piece of cookie or a potato chip, don't. Sweet, oily foods will spoil their appetite for the nutritious food they need to stay healthy and even make them sick.

The easiest way to feed your gerbils is to scatter the seed or pellets on the bedding. Gerbils are burrowing animals. They cannot burrow very far in the aquarium because the bedding isn't very deep, but they constantly dig, anyway. They will easily find and eat whatever food they need.

How much food does a gerbil need? If you are using seed, add two or three tablespoons each time the bedding is replaced—about every two weeks. Then every day add a teaspoonful for each gerbil in the cage. If you are using food pellets, follow the manufacturers' recommendation. Remember also to use common sense. If some pellets are always left uneaten, cut back. If the pellets

are always consumed, try increasing the amount just to be sure your animals have enough.

If your family goes away for a few days, place an extra portion of dry food in the cage for each day you'll be gone and make sure the waterer is full. Then enjoy your vacation. Your gerbils will be just fine. If you are going to be gone longer than a week, ask a friend to "gerbil-sit."

Toys for gerbils
Some people complain that gerbils don't do anything—they just sit or sleep all day. The problem is not with the animals but with their owners. It's not enough to give your pets food and water; it's also your responsibility to play with them and give them something to do. One way to keep your gerbils active is to be sure they have some good toys.

Many toys are sold for small animals such as mice, gerbils, and hamsters. Most are made of plastic. If you buy plastic toys, keep in mind that they won't last long because your gerbils will chew them up. If you don't want to keep buying new ones, you might want to let the animals play with their plastic toys for just a half-hour or so each day.

If you are housing your animals in a standard ten-gallon aquarium tank, you can purchase a plastic "entertainment center" that will fit into it. This apparatus consists of a lid to which a variety of tubes can be fitted. The tubes can be connected to form different shapes and patterns. Other equipment such as an exercise wheel or a "house" can be added. My gerbils love to run up and down and through the tubes. If the cover of the house is removed, they like to stand on their hind legs with their front legs draped over the edge, looking out at the world. They have never tried climbing out of the house, but your pets might be more adventuresome, so be prepared.

Gerbils love exercise wheels. Wheels without spokes, such as the one in the entertainment center shown here, are safe to use. But you must take precautions with metal exercise wheels. Such a wheel should never be used if there is more than one animal in the cage. An animal running on the wheel makes it spin very rapidly, and a second animal can be caught between the rapidly moving spokes and the stationary frame and be severely injured. Even one animal running by itself on the wheel can get its long tail caught.

I once saw a gerbil get its tail caught in a moving exercise wheel even though the animal was standing some distance from the wheel. The spokes not only cut off the tip of the tail but ripped off a good portion of the skin as well. The gerbil was in great pain, but luckily a veterinarian was able to save its life.

There are many gerbil toys you can make or find around the house. What could be simpler than just setting the screen cover of the cage on end, inside the cage? My gerbils love to climb up and down this "hill."

Anything that serves as a tunnel will provide gerbils with hours of pleasure. You might use a tin can with both ends removed (be sure there are no sharp edges) or cardboard tubes from paper towels or toilet tissue (be sure the tissue is unscented, as the perfume may make the gerbils sick). My gerbils play the tunnel game for hours—in one end and out the other. Then they chew the tube to shreds or crawl inside and go to sleep.

My gerbils also like to play in empty tissue boxes and chew on small sticks (unpainted, of course).

In case of fleas

If you watch a cage full of gerbils, you will notice that they spend a lot of time grooming both themselves and each other. Gerbils do not usually have fleas, ticks, lice, or other insect pests. But it is easy for a gerbil living in a pet store to pick up a pest from another animal. So as a precaution, you might want to use an insecticide when you first set up the cage. That way you'll be sure to kill off any insects that may have come home with the gerbils before these pests have a chance to reproduce and spread throughout the cage and your house.

A small can of flea spray is all you'll need. Read the label to be sure the insecticide can be used on small animals such as gerbils. Don't purchase an insecticide made for dogs—it will be much too strong.

Shop around

Before purchasing your gerbils, cage, and equipment, it is a good idea to visit several pet stores. Check the selection and cost of animals, equipment, and supplies. Be sure to note which store is the cleanest and seems to give its animals the best care. If possible, plan to buy your pets there even if they cost a little more.

Check with your parents

Gerbils are very friendly and gentle, but all animals, wild or pet, sometimes bite. Before buying my pets, I visited my doctor and got a tetanus shot. It only hurt a little. Your parents might want to check with your doctor to see if you should get one, too.

You and your parents should also decide whether to buy two males, two females, or a male and a female gerbil.

Two male or two female gerbils in one cage are ideal pets. They will entertain each other and provide their owners with hours and hours of pleasure with a minimum amount of care.

Buying a male and a female and keeping them together in one cage means that you are soon likely to have a cageful of babies. Breeding gerbils is very interesting and educational. But before you begin, talk to your parents. See how they feel about allowing your gerbils to have just one litter. (A litter may be one to twelve babies.)

Even if you decide to breed your gerbils just once, you still must find homes for the babies. Ask your friends, relatives, and classmates. Sometimes pet stores will take baby gerbils if you don't expect to get paid for them.

It's important to have homes lined up *now*, even before you buy your gerbils.

Setting up the cage

As soon as you have purchased your pets, you will want to put them into their new home. You can do this if you have the cage ready before you go to the pet store.

If you haven't already done so, try lifting the empty cage. Can you handle the weight without straining? If not, ask for help.

Wash the aquarium inside and out with a soft sponge, using a low-sudsing detergent and water. After rinsing off all the soap, dry the cage with paper towels. If the aquarium has been used by any other animal, add a bleach such as Clorox to the wash water.

After the cage is dry, lightly spray insecticide into the four corners and one or two spots in the center of the floor. (The instructions on the can of insecticide will probably say to spray the animals directly, but I don't like doing this because it's easy to spray in their eyes.) Remember to wash your hands after using the flea spray. You should use it the next two or three times you clean the cage, but after that it shouldn't be necessary, as long as your pets aren't exposed to other animals.

When the insecticide is dry, cover the floor with bedding—about an inch deep is fine. Wash and fill the waterer. Put food in the cage. Place two or three sheets of unscented tissue in one corner. Gerbils like to sleep in a bed or nest which they make out of whatever soft material is on hand. Your gerbils may shred the tissue to make a bed, or they may just scatter it around the cage. Either way, they will have a good time, and you will enjoy watching them.

Choosing your gerbils

Once your cage is ready and you've found a good pet store to deal with, it's time to buy your gerbils.

Pick animals with a color or color pattern that pleases you. In the wild, both male and female gerbils are reddish brown with whitish undersides. In the short time that people have been breeding gerbils, various colors and patterns have emerged, including dove gray, solid black, black and white, and reddish brown with patches of white. The names for these colors and patterns differ from breeder to breeder and store to store. The breeder from whom I purchased the pair of gerbils shown in this book said they were called "spotted" gerbils. The first babies produced by my spotted gerbils were not all marked like their parents. One had no white on its back, and one was black and white instead of reddish brown and white.

It is important that you select healthy animals. Each gerbil you choose should be active, friendly, and curious. It should come up to you when you approach the cage. Its eyes should be clear and bright; its fur should be smooth and shiny, covering its entire body (even the tail), with no bare spots. There should be no sores on the gerbil's snout, mouth, or any other part of its body. Nor should there be any sign of diarrhea, which is difficult to cure in gerbils.

Most gerbils are not offered for sale until they are about eight weeks old. At this age, any two animals (two males, two females, or a male and a female) will get along fine, even if they were not brought up together. At about twelve weeks, male and female gerbils begin to pair off. Some breeders and pet store owners will sell paired gerbils. Once gerbils mate, they stay together for the rest of their lives. If one dies, the other usually will not accept another mate.

After they are twelve weeks old, gerbils that have not mated and were not brought up together may not get along when placed in one cage. They may even fight until one is killed. When buying older gerbils, ask someone at the pet store to place them both in one cage to see how they get along. If they fight, try two other animals.

It is very difficult to tell young male and female gerbils apart, so let the clerk at the pet store do this for you. It's not so hard when the animals reach maturity at about ten weeks. You will then see that the genitals of the mature female are very close to the anus, and that both the anus and the genitals are surrounded by a *round* patch of dark hair. The genitals of the male are farther from the anus, and both the anus and genitals are enclosed in a *long, thin* patch of dark hair.

The first day at home

Someone at the pet store will probably put your gerbils into a small cardboard container. Once you get home, how will you get the gerbils from the container to their cage? Gerbils seldom bite, but yours are probably very frightened now, and if you reach into the box to remove them, one may nip at you in self-defense. The easiest and safest way to transfer the gerbils is simply to place the container on the floor of the

female 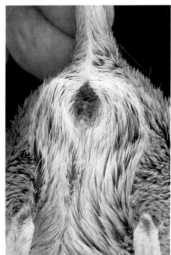   male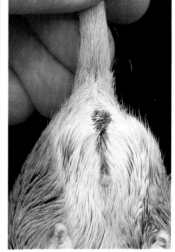

cage, open one end, and let them free.

Don't try to touch your new pets or make friends with them for a day or so. They will need some time to recover from their trip and to get used to their new environment.

Gerbil watching

This is a good time to observe your gerbils carefully. If they are about twelve weeks old, their bodies will be about three and a half inches long and so will their tails. Mature animals have bodies and tails that are about four inches long. My female gerbil was born with a tail that is very short—only about half the length of her body. This isn't normal, but I bought her anyway because she was a lovely, healthy animal in spite of her small tail.

A few very short, almost invisible eyelashes surround a gerbil's slightly bulging, jet-black eyes. Its mouth is set far back from its nose, and on either side of the mouth are whiskers which stick out about an inch. The ears stand upright except when the animal is frightened. Then they are pulled down flush against its head.

Although you can't easily see them, there are four teeth at the front of the mouth, two on top and two on the bottom. A gerbil also has twelve molars toward the back of its mouth, with a large gap between the molars and the incisors. The front teeth keep growing, and if they are not kept worn down, they can grow to such a length that they will interfere with eating and the gerbil will starve. In addition to supplying food pellets and dog biscuits for your gerbils to

front foot

back foot

chew, you can also give them small pieces of hard, clean wood and bones that won't splinter, such as thick beef bones. Bones are especially good because they also supply calcium.

The back legs and feet of a gerbil are much longer and stronger than the front ones. You can easily see this difference whenever one of your gerbils stands upright on its rear legs. Gerbils often stand this way to look around and check for predators. In this position, they look very much like little kangaroos! Their strong hind legs help gerbils to be very good jumpers. They can jump several feet forward, backward, sideways, or even straight up into the air to escape an enemy or just for fun.

Despite their small, weak front legs and feet, gerbils walk on all fours. They have five toes on both the front and rear feet, but the fifth toes or "thumbs" on their front feet are very short. The feet, including the toes, are covered with fur.

It's fun to watch a gerbil eat. It uses its front feet almost as if they were hands.

Because of their nice thick coats of fur, gerbils look heavy. But at four months, both my female and male gerbil weighed exactly the same, which was only four ounces. They were the same length—four inches. Although my male and female gerbils are the same size, males are often larger and heavier than females.

Gerbils have been seen to "thump" sometimes; that is, they brace themselves on their front feet and pound the ground with their back feet. This is done just before mating or when there is danger. I have never seen any of my animals thump. Perhaps this is because they are the only animals in the cage, they are well treated, and there is nothing hostile in their environment.

New friends

After a day or two you can begin to get acquainted. It's easy to make friends with a gerbil. Talk to it gently for a few minutes. Then slowly put your hand on the floor of the cage. The gerbil will come up to sniff it. Place some sunflower seeds in your palm, and pretty soon your gerbil will sit on your hand as it eats the seeds. Offer it a small piece of carrot, and the gerbil will remove the food so carefully that all you feel are whiskers brushing your fingers.

Picking up your gerbils

It is sometimes recommended that you pick up a gerbil by grabbing its tail near the base and quickly lifting the animal onto your other hand. I don't think this is the best technique. In order to catch a gerbil (or any animal) by the tail, you must move your hand rapidly, and this rapid hand movement may frighten it. Worse, if you accidentally grab the gerbil by the tip of the tail instead of the base, the skin at the tip may come off, causing the animal great pain.

Instead, I suggest you simply place your hand on the floor of the cage and wait until the gerbil sits on it. Then gently cup your hand around the gerbil and pick it up. If your gerbils don't like to sit on your hand, put an open clean tin can (with no sharp edges) on the floor of the cage. A gerbil loves anything that looks like a tunnel, and yours will soon crawl into the can. Cover the opening, pick up the can, and move the gerbil wherever you like. Don't move too quickly, though—think how that gerbil feels inside the can!

Playing with your gerbils

Remember that when working with any animal you must always be prepared for the unexpected. Before removing your gerbils from their cage, take precautions. Close the windows and doors to the room. Be sure there are no other animals around.

To reduce the risk of your gerbil injuring itself in a fall, position yourself over a table that has been covered with a folded blanket. Or sit on a blanket on the floor. If the gerbil falls it won't go far, and it will land on something soft.

Or you might play with your gerbil on top of the aquarium, on the wire-screen lid. Since a gerbil doesn't like heights, it shouldn't jump off. But keep in mind that a sudden movement or noise is all it takes to frighten any animal and cause it to jump or run away.

To train my gerbil to sit on my shoulder, I put a few sunflower seeds there. Then I took the gerbil out of the aquarium and placed it on the back of my left hand. It had nowhere to go except up my arm to the reward. I tried putting some seeds in my shirt pocket, but I couldn't get my pet to look there for the treat. Maybe you will have success with this trick.

You might enjoy building a maze and trying to train the gerbil to run through it a certain way. Or you could simply hold a sunflower seed in your fingers and see if your gerbil will sit up and beg like a dog.

Always remember to reward the gerbil with a sunflower seed when it does what you want. The more you talk to and handle your animals the better—three, four, or five times a day is not too often. Always be kind and gentle.

While it's fun to train gerbils, you don't have to. Many owners just enjoy watching their pets. As long as you have two gerbils, they will keep each other good company.

If a gerbil escapes
If a gerbil escapes, the first thing to do is to close the door of the room where the cage is kept, or the door to the *next* room, if you think the gerbil might

have gotten that far. This will keep people and other animals out and restrict your pet to one area.

The gerbil may do some exploring, but chances are it will want to come home pretty soon. If you sit on the floor, it may come right up to you and climb on your hand. Then you can pick it up and put it back in its cage. Or you can set the cage on its side and wait for the gerbil to crawl back in.

If the gerbil doesn't return soon, you can use a Havahart Animal Trap. These traps can capture an animal without hurting it at all. To test the trap, one evening I baited it with sunflower seeds and let a gerbil free. In the morning it was caught inside, unharmed.

Another gerbil-catching trick is to stack some books to form a stairway, put some sunflower seeds in a tall, slippery-sided container such as a wastebasket, and lean the container against the books. The gerbil will smell the food, climb up the books, and slip down into the "trap."

Some people deliberately let their gerbils run loose in a room, but I don't think that's a good idea. Gerbils like to chew on almost anything—furniture, books, wallpaper, rugs, clothes, wires. If you do decide to let your gerbils have the run of a room, or if one escapes and doesn't return soon, at least unplug and remove all electrical cords.

Starting a gerbil family

A gerbil couple may mate and produce a family any time after they are ten weeks old, but it may not happen until they are five or six months old.

One day you may see your male and female gerbils run wildly around the cage and then suddenly stop. The male will then mount the female. He will stay on her for only a few seconds. As soon as the two separate, each will bend almost in half as it washes its genitals. The chasing, mounting, and washing will be repeated, with breaks, over and over for a number of hours.

Before the chase, the male, and sometimes the female, may thump with its hind feet. The pair in this book did not do any thumping, but your animals may.

Mark the date of the mating on your calendar. If all goes well, twenty-four to twenty-six days later, the female will have babies.

If the female is pregnant, you will notice that as the days go by she will get bigger and bigger, but otherwise she will look and act normal. Be sure there is always a slight surplus of food in the cage so you know the mother has plenty to eat.

On the twenty-second or twenty-third day, give your mother-to be some soft material such as tissue so she can build a nest for her babies. (Never give your animals cotton. If swallowed, it can make them sick.) Because I wanted to photograph the birth of the baby gerbils, I did not give my pregnant female any nesting material until after the babies were born. This didn't seem to harm the mother or babies in any way. After I photographed the birth, I put two sheets of tissue in the cage. Both the mother and father tore them into pieces and made a nest for the family.

The birth of the babies
Before giving birth, the female goes through a stage called *labor*. During this time many changes occur in her body in preparation for the babies to travel through the *birth canal* and *vagina*.

During labor the male and female separate. The female retires to a corner of the cage or to the nest and stays there. The male stays mostly on the other side of the cage.

All of my gerbils have given birth in the morning, between six and ten A.M., so it was easy to watch. If you are around when the babies are born, just watch—don't touch.

Each baby emerges from the vagina in a thin membrane or sac. You may see a little blood, but this is normal. The mother reaches back, grabs the sac, and places it in front of her. She rips the sac open, releasing the baby. Sometimes she will eat the sac and then gently wash the baby with her tongue. Other times she will wash the baby and then eat the sac. Some babies are active from the moment of birth. Others lie very still for what seems like minutes before they finally begin to twitch and move. This is all normal—don't worry. Just look but don't touch.

After each baby is born, the *placenta*, or afterbirth, emerges from the vagina. This is the tissue that surrounded and nourished the baby while it was inside the mother. She may eat this, too.

Most baby gerbils are strong and able to crawl away from the mother even while they are being washed. This is helpful, for while there may be as long as thirty minutes between births, sometimes the babies are born within minutes of each other, and the mother needs the room in front of her for the next baby.

In the photo on the right, you can see my mother gerbil's first three babies. Then the babies kept coming—six in all. A gerbil litter can consist of as few as one or as many as twelve; the average is five or six pups.

After all the babies were born (with a large litter this can take several hours), my new mother was tired and went into a corner of the cage to sleep. The new father stayed on his side of the cage. Some of the babies fell asleep wherever they happened to be, and others crawled around until they found a brother or sister. Then, snuggled next to a warm sibling, they too fell fast asleep.

Each new mother is different. One may stay in the nest, resting with her babies, another may get up and walk around, another may eat. In any case. leave both the mother and babies alone. If this is the mother's first litter, she won't quite know what to make of the babies. She may even pick one up and then drop it and walk away. Her mothering instinct hasn't yet come into play. Once again, don't touch. Soon she will gather the babies together in one corner of the cage or in the nest and cover them with her body to keep them warm.

It sometimes happens that a baby gerbil dies. Then you must remove it from the cage. (Ask your parents to help you with this.) Don't feel too sad. It's likely the baby wasn't healthy enough to survive, and nothing you could have done would have made a difference.

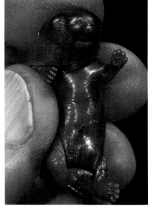

What dad does

Up to now the father has stayed away from the mother and babies, but once the babies are nursing, he carefully approaches the mother and joins her in the nest. From now on, the whole family—mother and father and babies—all live and sleep together.

For the next three or four weeks, the father helps with the care of the babies. He cleans them and keeps them warm when the mother is away eating or playing.

But having the father gerbil around can cause a problem. Very soon after the birth of the first baby, the female can mate again. She can have another litter in about twenty-four days, even while nursing the first litter. If this happens, you will have a very large gerbil family indeed!

Because I wanted to take photographs of a gerbil family acting more or less the way they would in nature, I left my male and female together. But to prevent your female gerbil from having another litter, *you must remove the male as soon as the female goes into labor.* You will have to put him in a separate cage or find a new home for him.

Watching the babies grow

ONE DAY OLD: Gerbil babies are very small and weigh almost nothing. This newborn weighed 2.8 grams. That's less than an eighth of an ounce, even less than the weight of a penny.

When first born, a baby gerbil is about 3.7 centimeters or one and a half inches long, not including its tail. Its skin is dark pink, almost red. Its eyelids are shut tight, and the openings in its ears are plugged, so it is both blind and deaf. The ears lie flat against the head as if they are glued there. The baby gerbil has no visible body hair, but it does have short, almost transparent whiskers. Its legs are strong enough so that it can raise its body and move about in a sort of swimming motion. There are tiny nails on the front and back feet.

Very soon the babies crawl to the mother, find nipples, and begin to nurse. To allow the babies to reach her nipples, the mother stands and lifts her body. Only occasionally does she lie on her side.

A gerbil mother has only six nipples. If she has a large litter, she often builds two nests. She keeps some of the babies in each, going back and forth from nest to nest to feed them. That way the babies do not have to fight for a nipple. If you see your mother moving some of her babies to a different corner of the cage, she is not discarding them but is getting ready to make a second nest.

Nursing babies place a great drain on the mother's body, so be sure to put extra food in the cage.

TWO DAYS OLD: At last the baby weighs 3.6 grams—as much as a penny. And if you look closely, you can see body hair beginning to grow.

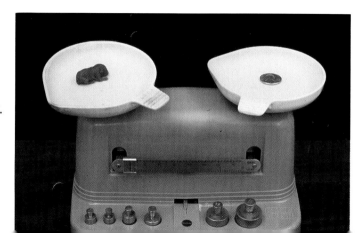

35

FIVE DAYS OLD: The body hair is now well developed, and the little gerbil's ears have lifted off its head. Its whiskers show up well in this photo.

Every so often, for reasons I could not figure out, the mother or father gerbil violently tore the nest apart, scattering the babies in all directions. Then both parents worked to rebuild their home, although they were not exactly coordinated. One would start to return the babies while the other was still piling up tissue, and soon several children were covered by nesting material! But the babies quickly crawled out, and no one in the family seemed upset by this upheaval.

SEVEN DAYS OLD: There's a lot of hair on the top of this youngster's body, but the underside still has very little growth. Although it's hard to tell for sure at this age, I'd guess this gerbil's fur will be black and white.

A baby gerbil's life consists mostly of nursing, sleeping, and being washed by its mother or father. Often I hear a lot of high-pitched squeaking coming from the nest, but it's hard to tell whether the noise is being made by the parents or the babies!

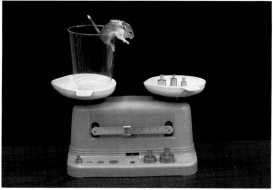

FOURTEEN to SIXTEEN DAYS OLD: The babies' fur is growing nicely, and now the coloring of each youngster can be seen. The ears are still small, but they are beginning to look like gerbil ears. The teeth are small but well developed, and though still nursing, the babies now chew on the bedding and seeds.

The little gerbils still spend most of each day sleeping and nursing. But at times they are very active, even though their eyes are still closed. As soon as one crawls away from the nest, they all crawl away. At first the parents chase after them and drag them back, but after a while they just give up and let the youngsters have the run of the cage. Even though they can't see, they don't bump into things. Their long whiskers help them to feel their way. And when they are tired or hungry, their strong sense of smell leads them back to the nest for food and warmth and companionship.

The babies are so lively that I have to place each in a container to be weighed. This youngster weighs 8.8 grams, about three times its birth weight.

EIGHTEEN DAYS OLD: The youngsters' eyes are finally beginning to open—the little rascals are really active now!

37

TWENTY-ONE DAYS OLD: Now the average weight of the young gerbils is 12.2 grams. They are so active that they can climb right out of the container while they are being weighed. They chew on everything, from seed to wood shavings. The parents no longer bother to rebuild the nest, but they still wash their babies often, and the whole family sleeps together.

TWENTY-FOUR to TWENTY-EIGHT DAYS OLD: The youngsters explore everywhere in the cage. They have found the waterer and have learned to drink from it. They will now play with almost anything. They especially like paper tubes, plastic toys, or a tin can. I set the cover from a small aquarium on an angle, and they had hours of fun and exercise as they ran up and down it. I put a small board on the bedding, and they built tunnels under it. When one went under, another came out—almost as if they were taking turns.

The young gerbils are starting to eat solid food. They quickly learn to sit on their rumps and eat with their hands. When you see your young gerbils eating solid food, be sure to increase the amount of seed you place in the cage each day. Add an extra teaspoonful of seed for each gerbil, or more pellets, according to the manufacturer's directions. If some seed and one or two pellets are left each day, you'll know you are adding enough.

Nursing can continue for another

week or two. But if you suspect the mother is going to have another litter, the babies first should be weaned because the mother needs to build up her strength. The easiest way to wean the first litter is to move the mother, rather than the children, to a new cage.

TWENTY-EIGHT DAYS on: You can now introduce your young gerbils to fruits and vegetables. The favorite green of my young gerbils is fresh dandelion leaves. I put several pieces of dandelion leaf into the cage, but if there isn't enough to go around, two gerbils grab a piece back and forth from each other. Usually, they end up eating from opposite ends of the same leaf.

You can start to train your gerbils informally when they are first born. Every time you are near the cage, talk to them so they will get used to the sound of your voice. Once they leave the nest, put your hand into the cage every day and let them sniff it and walk over it. Soon they will accept you as part of their world.

Now you can begin more active training. When a young gerbil sits on your hand, lift it a few inches and allow the gerbil to walk from one hand to the other. When the gerbil is used to doing this, you can remove it from the cage, keeping it just a few inches above the table or floor in case of a fall. Watch how still it stays as it looks around and studies the world!

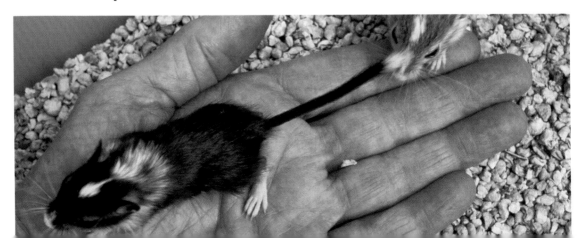

More gerbil babies?

At six weeks, most babies no longer nurse. They can go to new homes when they are eight weeks old.

Although many females don't become pregnant until they are about five or six months old, a female can give birth at ten to twelve weeks and have a new litter as often as every month. The average female has about five pups in each litter and about seven litters in her lifetime. And of course all the females in these litters can have babies of their own! You can see that in a short time you could be overrun by gerbils. To avoid this problem, you must separate the males from the females before they are ten weeks old.

Place all the females in one cage and all the males in another. (If you have trouble telling the sex of your gerbils, ask a veterinarian or someone at a pet store to help you.) Since all these animals have been living peacefully together, they should accept this arrangement. You might decide now to keep just two females or two males and send the rest to good homes.

If a gerbil gets hurt

Gerbils occasionally have accidents. Probably falls and fights account for most of the injuries. Both can be prevented to a great extent.

Falls great enough to cause an injury occur only outside of the cage, and you can prevent these falls by playing with your gerbils over a table or near the floor.

Like most animals, gerbils will fight to protect their territory. If you introduce a new gerbil into the cage, the "home" gerbils may fight it. Be prepared with a stiff piece of cardboard. If a fight starts, don't reach in with your bare hands to separate the animals. Instead, push the cardboard between the two animals and remove the stranger.

Sometimes fighting can be prevented by placing both animals in a new cage. Then neither "owns" any territory to protect. Another approach is to divide a cage in two by setting a barrier in the middle and placing a gerbil on either side. After a day or two, the gerbils will get used to each other's odor and accept each other.

If, in spite of all your precautions, a gerbil is injured, you should wear leather gloves to pick it up. The animal is likely to be frightened and in pain, and it may turn on you.

If the injury looks serious, immediately call a veterinarian. It's best to find a veterinarian who works with small animals, but any vet can probably give you good advice.

If the injuries seem minor, simply wash the wounds with a mild antiseptic. Don't bother putting on bandages because the gerbil will just remove them. Place the patient in a cage by itself, give it some food and water, and set the cage in a warm, quiet place. If the gerbil isn't back to its normal self in two days, contact a vet.

If a gerbil gets sick
If one of your gerbils is less active than usual and seems to be staying by itself in a corner of the cage, it may be sick. Diarrhea, sores, or loss of appetite are other indications of illness. You should move a sick gerbil to a temporary home to isolate it from the other gerbils. Give it a little extra care, and it may easily recover by itself.

Be sure the sick animal's cage is in a warm location, although the temperature shouldn't be over eighty-five degrees. Give the patient clean water and its usual food. You can even give it fresh food, but be sure to remove promptly what the gerbil doesn't eat.

If the gerbil hasn't recovered in two days, get in touch with a veterinarian.

The best way to keep your gerbils healthy is to follow these rules:

1. Watch your gerbils' diet. Feed them a balanced diet of fresh, healthy food. Don't give them human snack foods. Remove uneaten fresh food from the cage.

2. Replace the water and clean the waterer regularly.

3. Keep the cage clean.

4. Keep the temperature of the cage comfortable. Be especially careful that it doesn't get too hot in the summer.

5. Don't let people with colds near your gerbils.

6. Don't add a new gerbil to the cage unless it has been quarantined for at least seven days.

When a gerbil dies

A gerbil's life span is approximately three years. It's a hard thing to face, but death is a part of life, and sooner or later your animals will die.

If a gerbil becomes sick and the veterinarian tells you there is no chance of recovery, you might decide to ask the vet to put your pet to sleep. This is called *euthanasia,* which means a painless, peaceful death. The vet or the animal shelter can perform this service. The vet will dispose of the body, or you can ask him or her to give it to you so you can bury your pet yourself. You might want to talk to your parents about this decision, which isn't ever easy. If you decide to let your animal die naturally, ask the vet what you can do to make its last days as comfortable as possible.

It is natural to feel sad when a pet dies. You may feel a little better if you think about all the good times you and your gerbil had together.

Photographing your gerbils

With so many cameras and cam recorders available today, you may want to record your pets. While a glass aquarium makes a good home for small animals, getting good pictures of pets in a glass cage is difficult. When we look at an animal in an aquarium, our mind blocks out all of the reflections and all the objects in front of and behind the aquarium. We see only what we want to see—the animals. But a camera records *everything*. It will not only see the animal but what surrounds the aquarium. It will also photograph the aquarium itself and everything that is reflecting off the large pieces of glass that form its sides, including the photographer and his or her shiny camera!

It isn't easy for a photographer to produce a photograph that imitates what the mind sees. To eliminate all reflections from the photos I took for this book, I built a "black room" by hanging four eight-foot-long black drapes from the ceiling. Inside this black room I put a wooden table with the aquarium on it. To take the photos, I dressed in black and used an all-black camera, with no shiny chrome trim.

The camera I used was a seventeen-year-old *non*–auto-focusing Nikon with a 105mm true macro lens. (An auto-focusing camera would focus on the front surface of the glass facing the camera, and the animals, somewhere inside the aquarium, would be out of focus.)

You're welcome to set up your photos as I did, but it would be easier if you

just took your gerbils out of the glass aquarium and set them on the screen cover. Without the glass to worry about, you can use an auto-focusing camera plus a flash that's mounted on or built into the camera.

If you haven't trained your animals to be outside the aquarium, try photographing them in a bird cage that's been painted black.

Because new models of cameras and cam recorders are being introduced almost monthly, it's hard to give up-to-date advice on what kind of equipment to buy. But if you would like to buy a camera, here are some things to think about.

Before you go to a camera store, make a list of the kinds of subjects you would like to photograph in the next two or three years. It would be foolish to purchase an expensive professional camera if you're planning just to take snapshots of your friends. If you're planning to take more challenging shots, you must get the right kind of equipment. A camera and lens needed to photograph a flower close up would not be the right camera to take to an auto race.

Talk to a clerk about your needs and listen to his or her suggestions. Then go home and think about what you've learned. I make it a point never to buy a piece of equipment on my first trip to a store but instead to return in a day or two after I've had time to make a wise decision.

The latest equipment is not necessarily the best, and you should consider buying used equipment. A three-year-old camera that has had only fifteen to twenty rolls of film put through it is, in my opinion, still a new camera, and if it sells for half the price of a new camera, it should be seriously considered.

Enjoy photographing your gerbils!

46

Index

About the Author   Jerome Wexler was introduced to photography by his ninth-grade science teacher in an after-school camera club. He has been a professional photographer since 1946 and has had approximately fifteen thousand photographs published all over the world.

Mr. Wexler's photos have always been used for educational purposes. He first worked as an agricultural photographer, taking pictures of all kinds of farming activities as well as good and bad farming practices. The photos were used in advertisements, farm journals, magazines, and textbooks.

What he loves to do most is illustrate—with photographs—children's books on plants, animals, and insects. *Pet Gerbils* is his thirty-eighth such book. Many have received honors and awards; some have been translated and republished in Japan, China, Germany, Finland, Sweden, Holland, and Great Britain.

Both the Smithsonian Institution and the Agricultural Photo Library, a division of the United States Department of Agriculture, have asked Mr. Wexler to consider leaving them his vast collection of thirty-seven thousand photographs.